MEET ALBERT PUJOLS

Baseball's Power Hitter

Ethan Edwards

PowerKiDS press

New York

Published in 2009 by The Rosen Publishing Group, Inc.
29 East 21st Street, New York, NY 10010

First Edition

Editor: Amelie von Zumbusch
Book Design: Greg Tucker
Photo Researcher: Jessica Gerweck

Photo Credits: Cover, pp. 5, 7, 8, 10, 12, 14, 16, 17, 18 (main), 18 (inset), 20, 21, 22, 23, 24, 27, 29, 32 © Getty Images; p. 9 by GeoAtlas; p. 26 © MLB Photos via Getty Images.

Library of Congress Cataloging-in-Publication Data

Edwards, Ethan.
  Meet Albert Pujols : baseball's power hitter / Ethan Edwards. — 1st ed.
      p. cm. — (All-star players)
  Includes index.
  ISBN 978-1-4042-4487-0 (library binding)
  1. Pujols, Albert, 1980– —Juvenile literature. 2. Baseball players—Biography—Juvenile literature.
I. Title.
GV865.P85E39 2009
796.357092—dc22
[B]
                                2008000680

Manufactured in the United States of America

Contents

Meet Albert Pujols   4

From Santo Domingo to Independence   6

The 402nd Pick   11

The St. Louis Cardinals   13

Batting Champion   15

MVP   19

World Series Champions   21

The Other Albert Pujols   25

In the Coming Years   28

Stat Sheet   30

Glossary   31

Index   32

Web Sites   32

Albert Pujols is one of baseball's most talented sluggers, or hitters. He has hit hundreds of home runs in his career as a major-league baseball player. He is also one of the most dependable batters in baseball today. In fact, many people say Pujols is one of the best sluggers ever to play the game.

Pujols is the first baseman for the St. Louis Cardinals. He is an excellent **athlete** who values hard work. Pujols is also one of today's most popular and well-liked baseball players. He has many nicknames. One of his nicknames is El Hombre. *El hombre* means "the man" in Spanish.

All-Star Facts

Some of Pujols's other nicknames are The Machine, Phat Albert, and Prince Albert. One sports journalist, or reporter, even called him Winnie the Pujols.

Pujols is well liked by both his fellow players and baseball fans.

From Santo Domingo to Independence

Albert Pujols was born in a city called Santo Domingo in the Dominican Republic. The Dominican Republic is a country in Latin America. Many famous baseball players, such as David Ortiz and Pedro Martínez, have come from the Dominican Republic.

Pujols's father's name is Bienvenido. He was a famous **pitcher** in Dominican baseball. As baseball players do, Bienvenido Pujols often had to travel. Albert was raised by his grandmother, America, when his father was away.

All-Star Facts

Pujols was born on January 16, 1980. His full name is actually José Alberto Pujols.

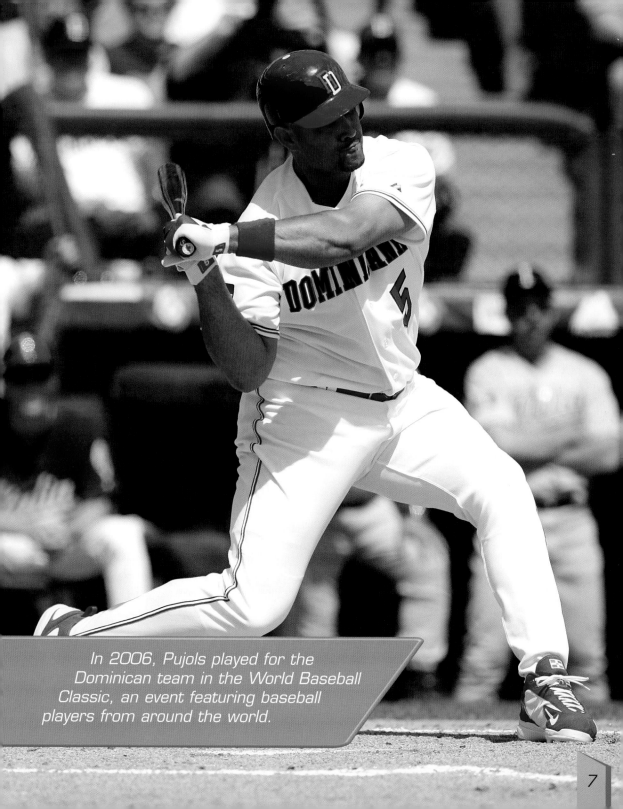

In 2006, Pujols played for the Dominican team in the World Baseball Classic, an event featuring baseball players from around the world.

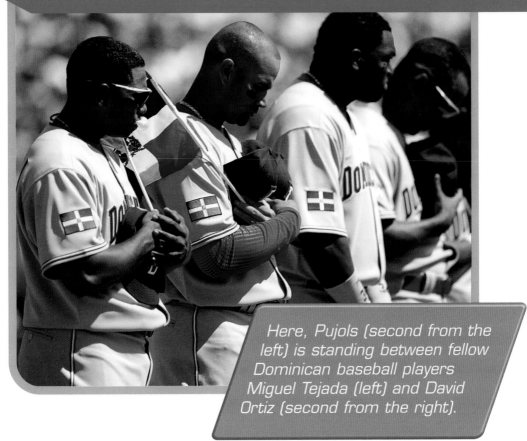

Here, Pujols (second from the left) is standing between fellow Dominican baseball players Miguel Tejada (left) and David Ortiz (second from the right).

When Albert was 16, he and Bienvenido moved to the United States. They lived in Independence, Missouri. Albert attended Fort Osage High School. He played baseball on his high-school team and fell in love with the sport.

In his first **season** of high-school baseball, Albert Pujols's batting average was over .500. A batting average is a special number in baseball that keeps track of how well a player hits. A .500 batting average means that Pujols got 5 hits in every 10 tries. A batting average around .280 is considered pretty good. A batting average of .300 is excellent. Pujols's average of .500 was amazing!

Santo Domingo, the city in which Albert Pujols was born, is the capital city of the Dominican Republic.

After he was drafted, Pujols played in the minor leagues for one season before joining the Cardinals.

The 402nd Pick

After high school, Pujols attended Maple Woods Community College. Maple Woods had a baseball team, and Pujols became the team's star. He was at Maple Woods for only one year, but in that year he batted .421 and even hit a **grand slam**!

Pujols was earning a **reputation** as a great young baseball player. Major-league teams sent scouts to watch him play. Scouts are baseball **experts** who look for talent in young players. Pujols entered the 1999 Major League Draft. The draft is the way teams select young players. Each team takes a turn in the draft.

The scouts **underestimated** Pujols's talent. Pujols was eventually drafted by the St. Louis Cardinals. He was the 402nd player selected. The Cardinals had no idea that number 402 would soon make baseball history.

Pujols hit a record-setting eight home runs in his first month as a major-league player!

The St. Louis Cardinals

In the spring of 2001, Pujols joined the Cardinals. Pujols got along well with his new teammates. Plácido Polanco, the Cardinals' second baseman, even became one of Pujols's best friends.

Pujols played so well in his first season that he was named to the National League's All-Star team. An All-Star team is made up of the best players at each position in one league. The All-Star teams from the National League and the American League play each other in a special game, called the All-Star Game, in the middle of the season. Playing in the All-Star Game is a big honor.

Pujols also helped his new team tie for first place in the National League Central Division. He hit 37 home runs that season. He hit 130 RBIs. "RBI" stands for "runs batted in." This means that the

Pujols (left) got along well with his new teammates, such as Cardinals' pitcher Darryl Kile (right).

Cardinals scored 130 runs thanks to Pujols's bat. Pujols hit more RBIs than any other rookie in the history of baseball! He was voted the 2001 Rookie of the Year.

Batting Champion

In the middle of the 2002 season, the Cardinals traded Pujols's good friend Polanco to the Detroit Tigers. Yet Pujols still played well in 2002. He batted .314 with 34 home runs and 127 RBIs. The Cardinals won the National League Central Division again, but they lost to the San Francisco Giants in the play-offs.

Pujols received lots of votes for the MVP, or Most Valuable Player, award. The MVP is the player who does more to help his team than any other player in the league. Pujols did not win the MVP, but he finished in second place to Barry Bonds.

All-Star Facts

Polanco and Pujols kept in touch and are still good friends. Pujols is the godfather of Polanco's son.

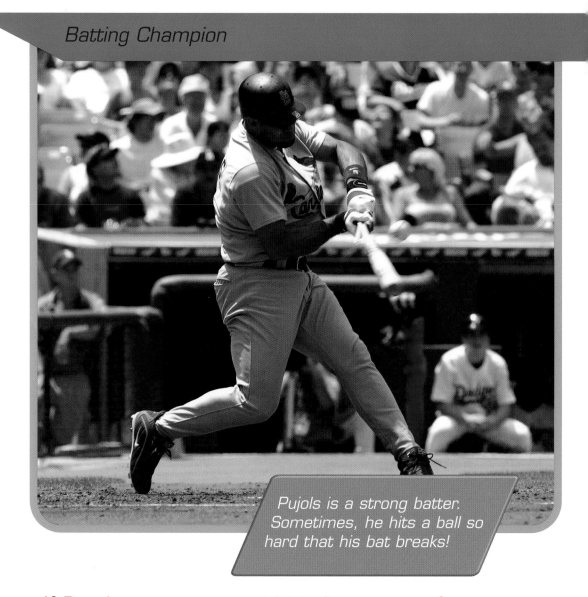

Pujols is a strong batter. Sometimes, he hits a ball so hard that his bat breaks!

If Pujols was great in 2002, he was on fire in 2003! He batted .359 with 43 home runs and 124 RBIs. Pujols became the youngest National League batting champion in over 40 years. The batting champion is the player with the best batting average at the end of the season. Pujols also led the National League in runs, hits, and doubles. He was only 23!

In 2003, Pujols (left) won the National League Hank Aaron Award. This award honors the league's best overall hitter.

During the 2004 season, Pujols **developed** plantar fasciitis. This is an extremely painful **injury**, also called policeman's heel. Pujols played through the pain. This gave him a reputation for being **tough**.

Even though he was injured, Pujols had one of his best seasons yet in 2004. He batted .331 with 46 home runs and 123 RBIs. He even helped the Cardinals reach the World Series. The World Series is baseball's championship. The World Series is to baseball what the Super Bowl is to football. Unfortunately, the Cardinals lost the World Series to the Boston Red Sox.

In 2005, Pujols batted .330 and hit 41 home runs and 117 RBIs. He helped the Cardinals reach

In 2004, Pujols became the Cardinals' full-time first baseman. Inset: Pujols cheered when the Cardinals won the National League Championship Series.

the play-offs again, but they lost to the Houston Astros in the National League Championship Series. However, baseball journalists agreed that Pujols had done more for his team than any other player in the National League. They voted to give him the National League MVP award!

ALBERT PUJOLS MVP!

On November 15, 2005, Pujols was named MVP, delighting this boy and many other Cardinals fans.

World Series Champions

In April 2006, Pujols set a record by hitting 14 home runs. No one had ever hit that many in the first month of the baseball season before! By this time, everyone agreed Pujols was a great slugger. However, many baseball experts and journalists thought he was not a very good fielder. He made a lot of errors at first base. Baseball errors happen when a player fails to make a routine, or simple, play.

Pujols worked hard to improve in the field. That hard work paid off, and Pujols won the Gold Glove Award in 2006. Gold Gloves are awarded every year to the best **defensive** players at each position.

In 2006, Albert Pujols became a much better defensive player.

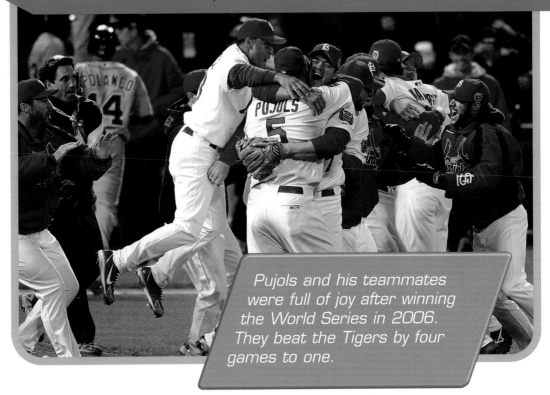

Pujols and his teammates were full of joy after winning the World Series in 2006. They beat the Tigers by four games to one.

The Cardinals had reached the **postseason** in four of Pujols's first five seasons. Unfortunately, the team kept falling short of winning the championship. In 2006, Pujols and the Cardinals reached the postseason again. This time, they faced the Detroit Tigers in the World Series. Pujols's old friend Polanco played for Detroit.

Pujols and Polanco both played well, but the Cardinals won. Pujols and the Cardinals were finally champions!

Pujols (left) and his son joined the Cardinals' managers and one of the team's owners to receive the World Series trophy, or award.

Deidre Pujols, who is seen here with her husband, is often called Dee Dee. She works closely with the Pujols Family Foundation.

The Other Albert Pujols

Baseball is very important to Pujols, but it is not the most important thing in his life. Pujols realizes that baseball is a game. Family and **compassion** are much more important to him.

Pujols married his wife, Deidre, on New Year's Day in 2000. Deidre already had a daughter, named Isabella. After he and Deidre were married, Pujols adopted Isabella. Along with Isabella, the Pujolses now have two other children, Albert Jr. and Sophia.

Isabella was born with a condition called Down's syndrome. Down's syndrome affects a person's **physical** growth and ability to learn. Albert and Deidre created a **charitable** organization called the Pujols Family Foundation. The foundation raises money to help people who have Down's syndrome and their families.

Albert Pujols loves spending time with his kids. He even brings his children, including baby Sophia, to watch some of his baseball games.

Though his charity work, family, and baseball keep him busy, Pujols found time to start his own business. In 2006, he opened a **restaurant** in St. Louis, called Pujols 5. Five is the number Pujols wears on his uniform.

Since Pujols was not born in the United States, he was not originally a citizen. However, Pujols enjoys living in the United States. He remembers the **poverty** he experienced growing up in the Dominican Republic and values the opportunities the United States offers. In 2007, Pujols became a U.S. citizen. He got a perfect score on the citizenship test!

Albert Pujols named his restaurant, Pujols 5, after the number he wears on his Cardinals uniform.

Pujols continues to break records. For example, his batting average was better than .300 in each of his first seven seasons. He also hit at least 30 home runs and 100 RBIs in each of these seasons. No other player in the history of baseball has accomplished these things. Most baseball players never achieve these numbers in a single season. Pujols has done it seven times in a row!

Many people respect Pujols for his great athletic skill and for his compassion. He is one of the most famous baseball players in the world. He has many more years of baseball left to play, but Albert Pujols is well on his way to becoming a baseball legend.

Albert Pujols is respected both for his great baseball skill and for his work in the community.

Stat Sheet

Height: 6' 3" (1.9 m)
Weight: 230 pounds (104 kg)
Team: St. Louis Cardinals
Position: First Base
Uniform Number: 5
Bats: Right
Throws: Right
Date of Birth: January 16, 1980

2007 Season Stats

At Bats	Runs	Hits	Home Runs	RBIs	Batting Average
565	99	185	32	103	.327

Career Stats as of 2007 Season

At Bats	Runs	Hits	Home Runs	RBIs	Batting Average
4,054	847	1,344	282	861	.332

Glossary

athlete (ATH-leet) Someone who takes part in sports.

charitable (CHER-uh-tuh-bul) Having to do with a group that gives help to the needy.

compassion (kum-PA-shin) Kindness.

defensive (dih-FEN-siv) Playing in a position that tries to prevent the other team from scoring.

developed (dih-VEH-lupd) Grew or formed.

experts (EK-sperts) People who know a lot about a subject.

grand slam (GRAND SLAM) A home run hit when there are teammates on every base.

injury (INJ-ree) Physical harm or hurt done to a person.

physical (FIH-zih-kul) Having to do with the body.

pitcher (PIH-cher) The baseball player who throws the ball for the batter to hit.

postseason (POHST-see-zun) The time after a regular sports season when play-off and championship games are held.

poverty (PAH-ver-tee) The state of being poor.

reputation (reh-pyoo-TAY-shun) The ideas people have about another person, an animal, or an object.

restaurant (RES-tuh-rahnt) A place where food is made and served.

season (SEE-zun) The group of games for a year.

tough (TUF) Strong or firm.

underestimated (un-dur-ES-tih-mayt-ed) Placed too low a value on.

Index

A
athlete, 4

D
Down's syndrome, 25

E
experts, 11, 21

F
family, 25–26

G
Gold Glove(s), 21
grand slam, 11

I
injury, 19

P
pitcher, 6
plantar fasciitis, 19
postseason, 22
poverty, 27

Pujols, Deidre
   (wife), 25

R
reputation, 11
restaurant, 26

S
scouts, 11
season(s), 8, 13,
   15, 17, 19,
   21–22, 28

Web Sites

Due to the changing nature of Internet links, PowerKids Press has developed an online list of Web sites related to the subject of this book. This site is updated regularly. Please use this link to access the list:
www.powerkidslinks.com/asp/pujols/